Flowchart Smart

THE SCIENCE OF GRASSLANDS

Richard and Louise Spilsbury

Gareth Stevens Publishing

Please visit our website, **www.garethstevens.com**.
For a free color catalog of all our high-quality books,
call toll free 1-800-542-2595 or fax 1-877-542-2596.

Cataloging-in-Publication Data

Names: Spilsbury, Richard. | Spilsbury, Louise.
Title: Grasslands / Richard and Louise Spilsbury.
Description: New York : Gareth Stevens Publishing, 2020. | Series: Flowchart smart | Includes glossary and index.
Identifiers: ISBN 9781538252222 (pbk.) | ISBN 9781538252239 (library bound)
Subjects: LCSH: Grasslands--Juvenile literature. | Grassland ecology--Juvenile literature.
Classification: LCC GB571.S65 2020 | DDC 551.45'3--dc23

First Edition

Published in 2020 by
Gareth Stevens Publishing
111 East 14th Street, Suite 349
New York, NY 10003

Produced for Gareth Stevens by Calcium
Editors: Sarah Eason and Harriet McGregor
Designer: Emma DeBanks
Picture researcher: Rachel Blount

Picture credits: Cover: Shutterstock: Shanvood (c), Irina Simkina (br); Inside: Shutterstock: A Lesik: p. 11t; Aaabbbccc: p. 5t; Andrzej_67: pp. 12-13; Aydngvn: p. 34b; Fiona Ayerst: pp. 20-21; Dmytro Balkhovitin: pp. 6-7; Traci Beattie: p. 15t; Radek Borovka: pp. 34-35; Chalintra.B: pp. 32-33; Tabor Chichakly: pp. 10-11; Delbars: pp. 44-45; Gdvcom: pp 28-29; Ghost Bear: p. 41t; Ken Griffiths: pp. 18-19; Roger de la Harpe: pp. 36-37; Harold House: pp. 26-27; Matt Jeppson: p. 23r; Ramona Kaulitzki: pp. 8-9; Lucag_g: p. 28b; LutsenkoLarissa: p. 6b; LynxVector: pp. 38-39; Leon Marais: p. 19t; Martha Marks: p. 13r; MPH Photos: pp. 1, 22-23; Orthgon: pp. 42-43; Milan Rademakers: pp. 4-5; Ragulina: pp. 14-15; Alicia Ramirez: p. 30b; Rosalie. S. Photo: pp. 40-41; Johan Swanepoel: p. 21t; Totsaa.arch Studio: pp. 24-25; Ttphoto: p. 44b; Vagabond54: pp. 30-31; Yhelfman: p. 27t; Bildagentur Zoonar GmbH: p. 36b; Zubik: pp. 16-17.

Printed in the United States of America

CPSIA compliance information: Batch #CW20GS: For further information contact Gareth Stevens, New York, New York at 1-800-542-2595.

Contents

Chapter 1

What Are Grasslands?

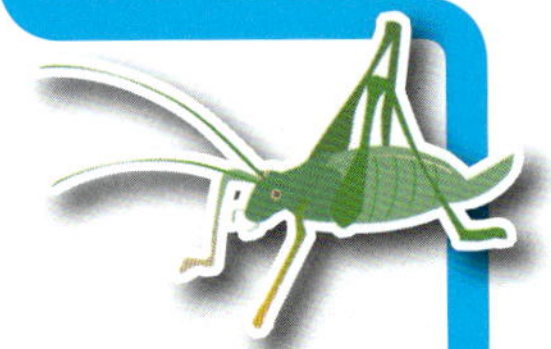

Grasslands are wide, open areas of flat or gently rolling land that are mainly covered in grass plants. Grasslands are huge and important **ecosystems**. They cover around 40 percent of all of the land in the world.

Grasslands grow in places where the soil is too poor or the weather too dry for most trees and many other plants to grow. In grasslands, grasses take over the land, cloaking it like a huge, green living carpet. Grasslands are often found between areas of **desert** and forest. They are found in places where the average annual rainfall is just enough to allow grasses, and in some places a few trees, to grow in the dry soils. In areas of grassland there is so little rain that there are also times of **drought** or wildfires, which prevent large forests from growing.

Rain in most grasslands is a rare sight. This grassland is in Kenya, Africa. Here, it rains only between March and May, and September and October.

An ecosystem is made up of living and nonliving things **interacting** with one another in an area. The living things include plants and animals, and nonliving things include weather, sunlight, water, and soil. All ecosystems have their own unique features. The grassland ecosystem includes everything in the grassland, from the tiniest insects and particles of dirt to huge grassland animals such as deer, elephants, and zebras.

This grassland is on the island of Madagascar, in the Indian Ocean. Around 75 percent of Madagascar is covered by grasslands.

Get Smart!

Grasslands are scattered across the planet. They are found on every continent except Antarctica. They are mainly located in the middle of continents, away from the coast. Almost half of the continent of Africa is covered with grasslands, the best known of which is the Serengeti, which covers 11,580 square miles (30,000 square km) of land.

Types of Grasslands

There are many different types of grasslands. The name given to grasslands changes, depending on where in the world they are located, but they can all be divided into two main groups: **tropical** and **temperate**.

Temperate grasslands are found in places with cold winters, warm summers, and very little rain all year round. In some temperate grasslands, there may be scattered trees and bushes among the grasses. These include prairies in North America, pampas in South America, and the steppe grasslands that stretch from eastern Europe to central Asia.

Other grasslands are found in tropical places where it is warm all year round. Tropical grasslands have a rainy season during which heavy rains fall, and a dry season, when it may not rain at all. Tropical grasslands have more trees and shrubs than temperate grasslands, and the grasses here are often taller. Tropical grasslands are also called savannas. They are mainly found in Africa, Australia, South America, and India.

Get Smart!

Grassland grass has two real seasons: a growing season and a **dormant** (nongrowing) season. In temperate grasslands, grasses stop growing during the cold months. In tropical grasslands, grasses are dormant in the dry months of the year. When grass plants are dormant, they die back to their roots. They stay alive, using energy stored in their roots. The soil around the roots protects them from the cold of winter or dry conditions. When days grow warmer or the rainy season begins, the grass plants grow new shoots, stems, leaves, and flowers.

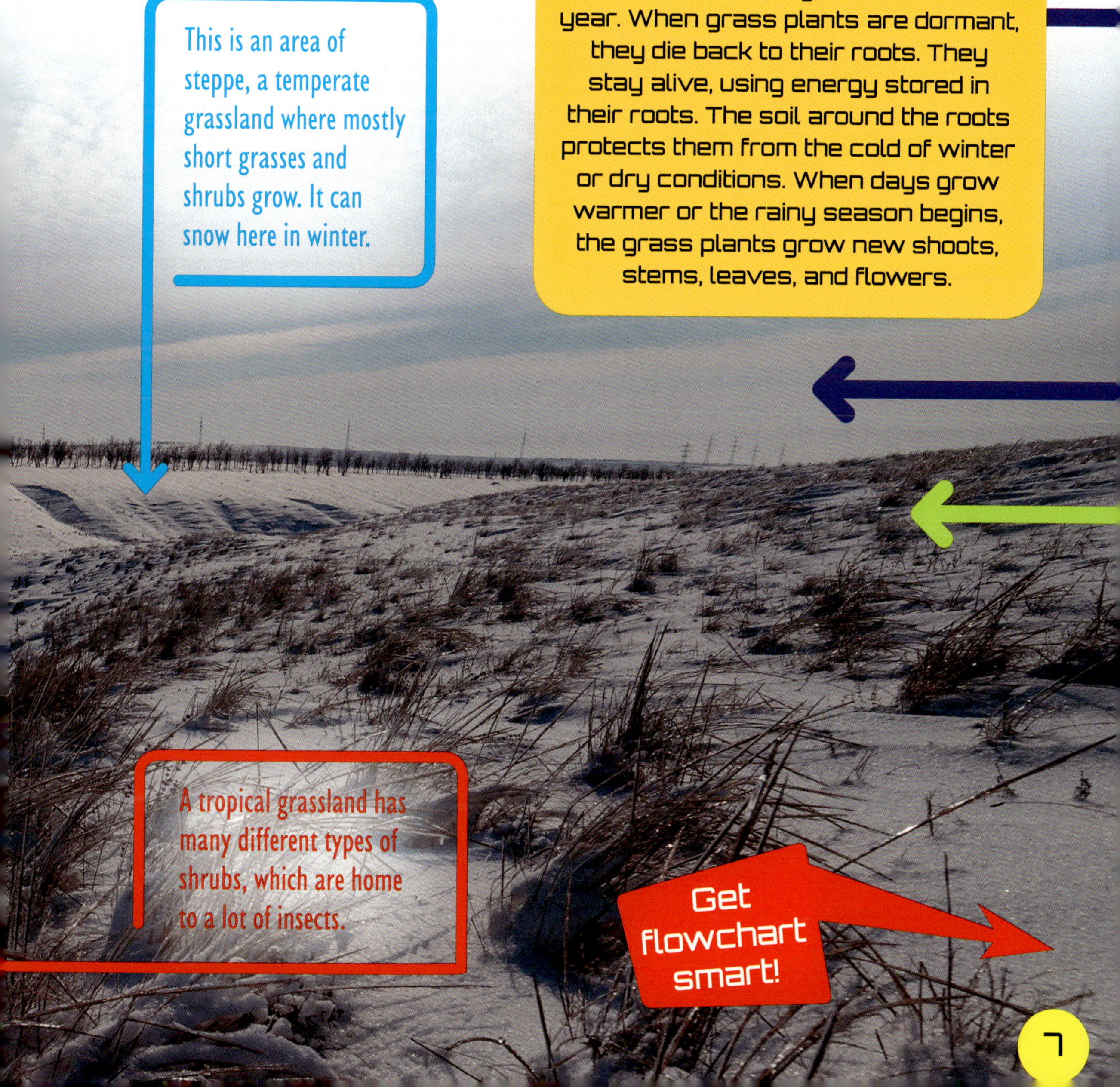

This is an area of steppe, a temperate grassland where mostly short grasses and shrubs grow. It can snow here in winter.

A tropical grassland has many different types of shrubs, which are home to a lot of insects.

Get flowchart smart!

How Grassland Grasses Grow

Let's look at the growing patterns of a grassland grass plant.

Grassland grass plants have two main seasons: a growing season and a dormant season.

The soil around the roots protects them from the cold of winter or dry conditions.

When days grow warmer or the rainy season begins, the grass plants burst into life. They grow new shoots, stems, leaves, and flowers.

In temperate grasslands, grasses stop growing during the cold months. In tropical grasslands, grasses are dormant in the dry months of the year.

When grass plants are dormant, they die back to their roots.

Grasses stay alive using energy stored in their roots.

Flowchart Smart

Chapter 2

Grassland Plants

Grasses are very tough. They can survive in areas where many other plants cannot. They can cope with less water than most plants and are not killed when grassland grazers eat their leaves.

When grasses are nibbled or trampled by animals, their green leaves soon regrow. The reason for this is that while most plants grow from the tips of their leaves and stems, grasses grow from the base. That is why they can survive in grasslands while other more easily damaged plants cannot.

These American bison are eating grasses on the prairie near Denver, Colorado.

Another reason for a grass plant's success is the shape of its leaves. Grass leaves are long and they are curled or rolled slightly along their length. All plants lose water through their leaves, but rolled leaves reduce the surface area that is exposed to the wind and air. This reduces the amount of water that a grass plant loses every day, which helps it cope with dry weather. Grass plants also grow many shallow and deeper roots over a wide area. This means they can access rainfall as soon as it hits the ground and soaks into the soil.

Wildfires can spread across grasslands at speeds of up to 14 miles per hour (22 kph).

Get Smart!

In hot summers and during dry seasons, wildfires spread quickly in grasslands. Old, dead grasses are very dry, so they catch fire easily. Flames spread quickly from plant to plant, until soon an entire grassland can be ablaze. Grass plants grow from parts at or just below the ground, so they can grow back soon after a fire as long as their underground roots are not damaged. Wildifires kill most trees and other plants. Without wildfires, shrubs and trees could quickly begin to take over grasslands.

Prairie Plants

A variety of grasses and other plants grow on prairies, including a colorful array of flowering plants.

Purple needlegrass, wild oats, foxtail, ryegrass, and buffalo grass are a few of the grass types in a prairie. Ryegrass is a short, tufted green grass and wild oats are medium-height grasses with dull brown stems and seed heads. Large bluestem grass can grow to 10 feet (3 m) tall. It has blue-green stems with purple or green seed heads on top. It is also known as turkey grass, and many **species** of wildlife use big bluestem grasses for food and shelter.

The American pasqueflower is also known as prairie smoke. It has a covering of very long silky hairs, which catch the light when the sun shines through them.

Wildflowers grow well in temperate grasslands such as prairies. Flowers that you might find growing on grasslands include asters, blazing stars, goldenrod, sunflowers, milkweed, and wild indigo. Milkweed ranges in color from pink to bright orange and can grow up to 6 feet (2 m) tall. Wild indigo has deep blue flowers. Some insects, such as bees and butterflies, feed on the nectar, a sugary juice found in the center of many prairie flowers. Other insects or their young feed on specific plants, without which they could not survive.

This bird is resting on a tumbleweed plant. As the tumbleweed rolls and spreads its seeds, it is giving its offspring a better chance of finding suitable ground on which to grow.

Get Smart!

Tumbleweed is a plant sometimes seen on prairies. When this plant is fully grown, it breaks free from its roots. It dries out in the sun to become a tangled ball of lightweight stems that is easily blown along by the wind. As it moves, it scatters its seeds, so young tumbleweed plants can then grow in new places.

Savanna Plants

African savannas are home to a huge variety of wildlife including big cats such as lions and cheetahs. Savannas are covered with grass plants, but there are also patches of thick shrubs and some tall trees.

Grasses in savanna grasslands often grow in thick clumps during the rainy growing seasons. They may be short or, in wetter areas, very tall. Bermuda grass is a low grass that forms a thick mat over the soil. It puts out roots to spread across the ground. Elephant grass can grow up to 10 feet (3 m) tall with pointed leaves up to 3 feet (1 m) long. Its leaves have razor-sharp edges, so only small animals or those with very tough skins can go near it!

The baobab tree is one of very few trees that can survive on the savanna.

Get Smart!

Some savanna plants have smart ways of protecting themselves from animals that try to eat them while they are young, before they are fully grown and strong enough to survive. Euphoria plants contain a nasty tasting, milky sap and acacia trees have sharp thorns to deter wildlife.

A few types of trees are able to grow in a savanna ecosystem and cope with the periods of drought. Some grow near pools of water that form during rainy seasons. Others, such as acacia trees, store water in their tough stems and have small, leathery leaves to reduce the amount of water they lose through **evaporation**. The baobab tree is able to soak up vast amounts of water with its far-reaching roots during the rainy seasons. It stores the water in its enormous trunk, which swells to hold the water for use in times of drought.

Tall savanna grasses provide cover for grassland animals such as cheetahs. The cheetahs hide in the grass as they watch for **prey**.

Get flowchart smart!

How Fires Help Grasslands

Discover how wildfires help grassland ecosystems.

In hot summers and during dry seasons, wildfires spread quickly in grasslands.

Most trees and other plants are killed.

Fires help grasses in grasslands. Without wildfires, shrubs and trees could begin to take over the grassland.

Old, dead grasses are very dry, so they catch fire easily. Flames spread rapidly from plant to plant. An entire grassland can be ablaze very quickly.

Grass plants grow from parts at or just below the ground, so they can soon grow back after a fire as long as their underground roots survive.

Chapter 3

Animal Adaptations

Animals survive in their ecosystems by having special features to help them. These are called **adaptations**.

Some animal adaptations are behavioral, which means that animals have adapted by behaving in a particular way. For example, zebras, elephants, and kangaroos group together in **herds** to keep safe. This is because there are few trees and bushes to hide among in the wide-open spaces of the grassland. In a herd, most animals can have their heads down grazing on the grass, while a few others in the herd keep a lookout for **predators**.

Frilled lizards feed on insects and other small animals. When threatened, their frill can expand to 12 inches (30 cm) wide.

Get Smart!

Grasslands have wide-open spaces. This can make it difficult for animals to escape predators. Frilled lizards have a large, loose area of pleated skin that rests over their shoulders. If a predator appears, the lizard quickly raises and opens the frill to make itself look big and frightening. It also opens its brightly colored mouth wide and hisses loudly. This scares most enemies away.

An elephant can grip a branch, snap it in half, and then use it to brush away insects on its skin, or to scratch its own back.

Other adaptations are physical. An elephant's 6-foot (2 m) trunk is so strong and flexible that it can be used like a human arm. It uses its trunk to suck up and spray dusty soil over itself. A layer of dust works like sunscreen and helps prevent insect bites. At the end of the trunk there are two nostrils and pointed parts that can pick up things, just like human fingers can. They can grasp and remove a single leaf and place it into the elephant's hungry mouth. The elephant also uses its trunk to drink by sucking water into the trunk and squirting it into its mouth.

On the Move

Grasslands are often huge and open spaces. Animals have different adaptations to help them cross large areas of land.

Many grassland birds, such as meadowlarks, can fly over the land, keeping watch for insects and other prey animals below while in the air, safe from predators. Kangaroos use all four legs when walking, but when they need to move quickly, they hop on their powerful back legs. Using this bouncing run, they can travel at speeds of 30 miles per hour (50 kph) or more, and they can leap more than 26 feet (8 m) in a single jump.

A cheetah is adapted to run fast for short distances to catch prey. It can cover around 330 feet (100 m) in just 3.2 seconds. Its backbone bends easily and can arch up high when the cheetah's front feet touch the ground. This allows the back legs to stretch so far forward that they can land ahead of the front legs. Then the cheetah pushes off and springs forward again from its back legs. A cheetah's paws have grooved pads with claws that grip and dig into the ground, like the tread on a sprinter's running shoes, to help them run fast.

The cheetah is the fastest land animal in the world. Its legs are very long, which allows it to take huge strides.

In grasslands, moving fast to escape predators can make the difference between life and death.

Get Smart!

Many herd animals, such as wildebeest and zebra, travel thousands of miles to find grasses to eat. This takes so long that babies are sometimes born during the journey. These young animals must be able to keep moving as soon as they are born. Baby zebras are born feet first and have legs almost as long as an adult—they can walk and even run within an hour of birth.

Camouflage!

Some grassland animals use **camouflage** to blend in with grassland plants and dusty soils. Lacking trees, rocks, or other structures to hide behind, some use this to keep safe. Others use camouflage to help them find and attack prey.

This lioness is perfectly camouflaged among the grass of the savanna. It will stand still if a prey animal looks in its direction, to avoid being seen.

Lions have yellowish-brown fur, which is very similar in color to the dry grasses of the African savanna where they live. This camouflage helps lions hide among the grasses while they are hunting. Lions use color to hide, but they themselves are color blind. This might explain why zebras, which lions hunt, are black and white. Blending in with the color of grasses would not help zebras escape lions, which use their senses of hearing and sight to find prey.

The red milk snake's bright red markings make it stand out in the grassland. This should be a problem for an animal that can be eaten by coyotes and other predators. These nonpoisonous snakes are safe, however, because they have similar colors and patterns to the poisonous coral snake, which predators avoid. When threatened, red milk snakes may also vibrate their tail to create a sound similar to that of a rattlesnake.

A red milk snake kills its prey by wrapping its body around it and squeezing it to death.

Get Smart!

Kori bustards are large grassland birds. They feed and nest on the ground. They have brown feathers to camouflage them against dry savanna grasses. When the female kori bustard has eggs in its nest, it also throws grass over its back to ensure it is well hidden from predators.

Get flowchart smart!

How Cheetahs Run So Fast

Discover the secret of a cheetah's speedy run.

A cheetah is adapted to run at high speed over short distances to catch prey.

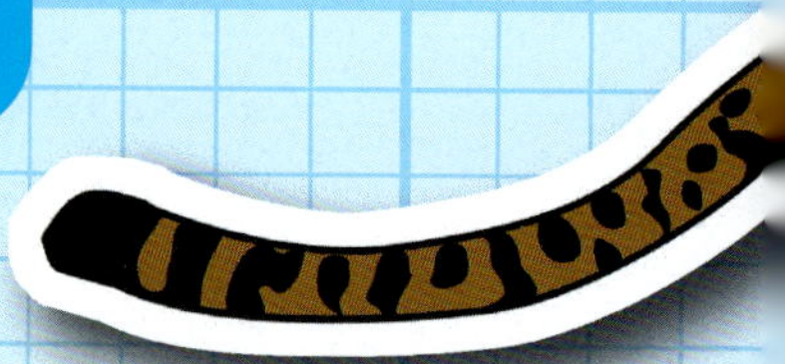

The cheetah's grooved pads have claws that grip and dig into the ground, like the tread on a sprinter's running shoes.

A cheetah's legs are very long, so it can take huge strides and cover the ground quickly.

Its backbone bends easily and can arch up high when the cheetah's front feet touch the ground.

Its high, arched back allows the cheetah's back legs to stretch so far forward that they can land ahead of the front legs.

Then the cheetah pushes off and springs forward again from its back legs.

Flowchart Smart

Chapter 4

Grassland Food Chains

The feeding relationships in an ecosystem are called a food chain. Like links in a chain, plants are eaten by insects, which are eaten by bigger animals, which in turn are eaten by even bigger animals.

Food chains begin with plants because plants trap energy from the sun, the source of energy for almost all living things on Earth. Plants use a green substance in their leaves called chlorophyll to trap the energy in sunlight. They use this energy to turn **carbon dioxide** gas from the air and water taken in through their roots into sugar. The plant stores the sugar in different parts of its body, from roots to leaves, to use later as food. This process is called **photosynthesis**. When a plant eater eats a plant, it gains the energy stored in the plant.

Many grassland plant eaters are adapted to get energy from grasses. Grasshoppers have large, flat mouthparts called mandibles. These help them chew through tough blades of grass. Some grassland birds such as prairie chickens scurry across the ground, feeding on leaves, fruit, and seeds as they go. Other birds are small and agile enough to climb up grass plants to feed on the seeds at the top. Butterflies have a long, hollow, straw-like mouthpart called a **proboscis**, which they uncurl and poke into the center of a flower to suck up the sweet, sugary nectar inside.

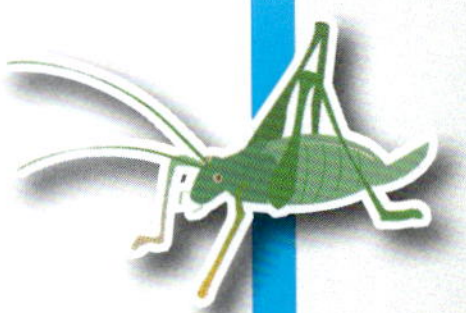

Grasshoppers use their long legs to hop from plant to plant to find food.

Jackrabbits use their strong front teeth to graze on different plants and their parts, from grasses to twigs. The plants provide the rabbits with water as well as food.

Get Smart!

Small, plant-eating grassland animals include jackrabbits, gophers, and mole rats. Jackrabbits eat grasses, flowering plants, and shrubs. Gophers and mole rats dig underground tunnels to eat roots and other underground plant parts.

Greedy Grazers

Large herds of animals graze on grasslands. They devour huge quantities of plant foods. There can be thousands of animals in a herd, so to ensure there is enough food to go around, different grazers are adapted to eat slightly different foods. This helps them share the grassland **resources**. For example, on the African savanna, long-necked giraffes eat leaves, buds, and fruit from the tops of trees such as acacias. Elephants eat lower leaves, bark, and branches, while zebras eat longer grass and stems. Gazelles and wildebeests eat mainly the shorter grass plants.

A fully grown adult male giraffe can eat about 145 pounds (65 kg) of food each day.

Grazers eat large quantities of grass because it does not contain a huge amount of **nutrients**. They need to eat a lot of it to survive. Grasses and other grassland plants can also be very tough to **digest**, and grassland grazers have different ways of dealing with this problem. Antelopes and bison have extra stomach chambers that help the animals digest the tough, fibrous plant parts. Ostriches peck up and swallow sand and small stones. These help grind up the grasses and other plant foods in their stomachs.

Get Smart!

A giraffe's neck is 6 feet (2 m) long. This helps it reach leaves at the tops of the trees. To feed safely from thorny acacia trees, a giraffe also has a very long, prehensile tongue. Prehensile means able to curl and wrap around objects and grip them tightly. Giraffes poke their tongue between thorns so they can grasp and pull off leaves and put them into their mouth. The tongue and inside of the mouth are also coated with tough skin as protection.

Ostriches eat insects as well as grasses and other plants. They only swallow when they have a large lump of food in their throat.

Predators

Grassland predators work in different ways to catch their prey. Some, such as the cheetah, work alone and use speed to chase down prey. Others, such as lions, stalk prey in groups before closing in on a herd and working in teams to trap individuals.

In pampas grasslands, pumas are the apex, or top, predators. No other animals eat adult pumas. Pumas stalk their prey, such as an armadillo, until they are close enough to leap on it and sink their huge teeth into the prey animal's neck. Pumas drag large prey to a hiding spot to feed on it at night. An armadillo uses its long nose to smell termites hiding in their muddy mound. Then the armadillo rips open the termite mound using its large middle toenails, and licks up the insects inside with its long, sticky tongue.

An armadillo's body armor cannot protect it from a hungry puma, which will eat—or try to eat—just about anything.

The coyote is an apex predator in a prairie food chain. A typical food chain here begins with big bluestem grass, which is eaten by grasshoppers. Grasshoppers are eaten by western meadowlarks. These birds nest and often feed on the ground, so they may fall prey to rattlesnakes. Rattlesnakes kill their prey quickly with a bite that injects venom, or poison. Coyotes hunt prey, such as a rattlesnake, alone, stalking it before they pounce and kill it with their powerful jaws and sharp teeth.

Get Smart!

Sometimes, several different animals eat the same foods. In African savannas, zebras, antelopes, and wildebeests all eat grass, and are all eaten by lions and hyenas. Many food chains linked together are called a **food web**.

Western meadowlark predators include skunks, foxes, hawks, coyotes, and raccoons.

Get flowchart smart!

A Prairie Food Chain

Let's follow the links in a prairie food chain.

Big bluestem grass traps energy from the sun and uses it to turn carbon dioxide and water into sugary food. This process is called photosynthesis.

Coyotes hunt the rattlesnake alone, stalking it before they pounce and kill it with their powerful jaws and sharp teeth.

A grasshopper uses its powerful jaws to bite through the tough big bluestem grass and then eat pieces of it.

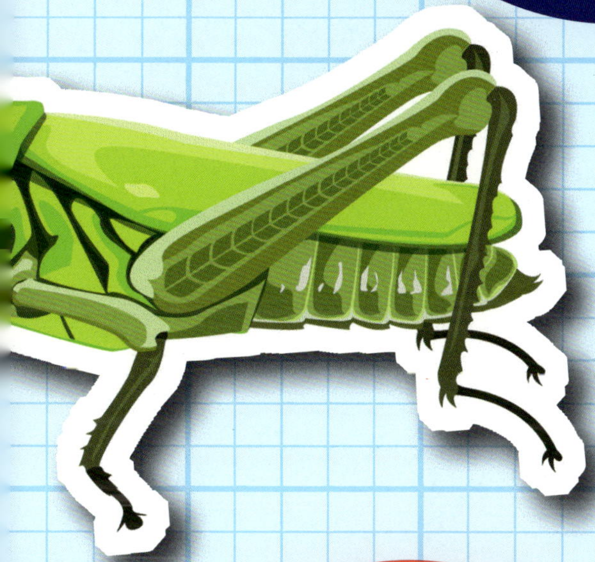

A western meadowlark snatches up the grasshopper in its sharp beak and eats it.

A rattlesnake quickly kills the meadowlark with a bite that injects venom.

Flowchart Smart

Chapter 5

Grassland Interactions

The ways in which different living and nonliving parts of a grassland interact with one another are vital to the health of the ecosystem. They are interconnected and rely on one another to survive.

Grassland ecosystems also have their own waste disposal system to help them keep healthy. **Decomposers** such as earthworms and **bacteria** feed on and break down waste and animal remains. This releases nutrients from the waste. Nutrients are substances that living things need to live. Rain washes the nutrients into the soil, where they can be used by grasses and other grassland plants to grow. By **recycling** nutrients, decomposers help new plants grow. These new plants prop up many grassland food chains and webs.

Other animals help keep grasslands healthy, too. Plains buffalo eat grass and walk long distances to find more grass. Their dung contains grass seeds. This helps spread the seeds away from the parent plants. The dung also contains nutrients, so it acts as a **fertilizer**, giving the seeds a better chance to germinate, or start to grow. When termites build their mounds, they help grasslands, too. Termites make holes as they dig through the ground and this allows rain to soak into the soil instead of running off the surface or evaporating in the heat. This encourages the growth of grasses, shrubs, and trees.

Grassland decomposers return nutrients to the soil from animal waste such as dung.

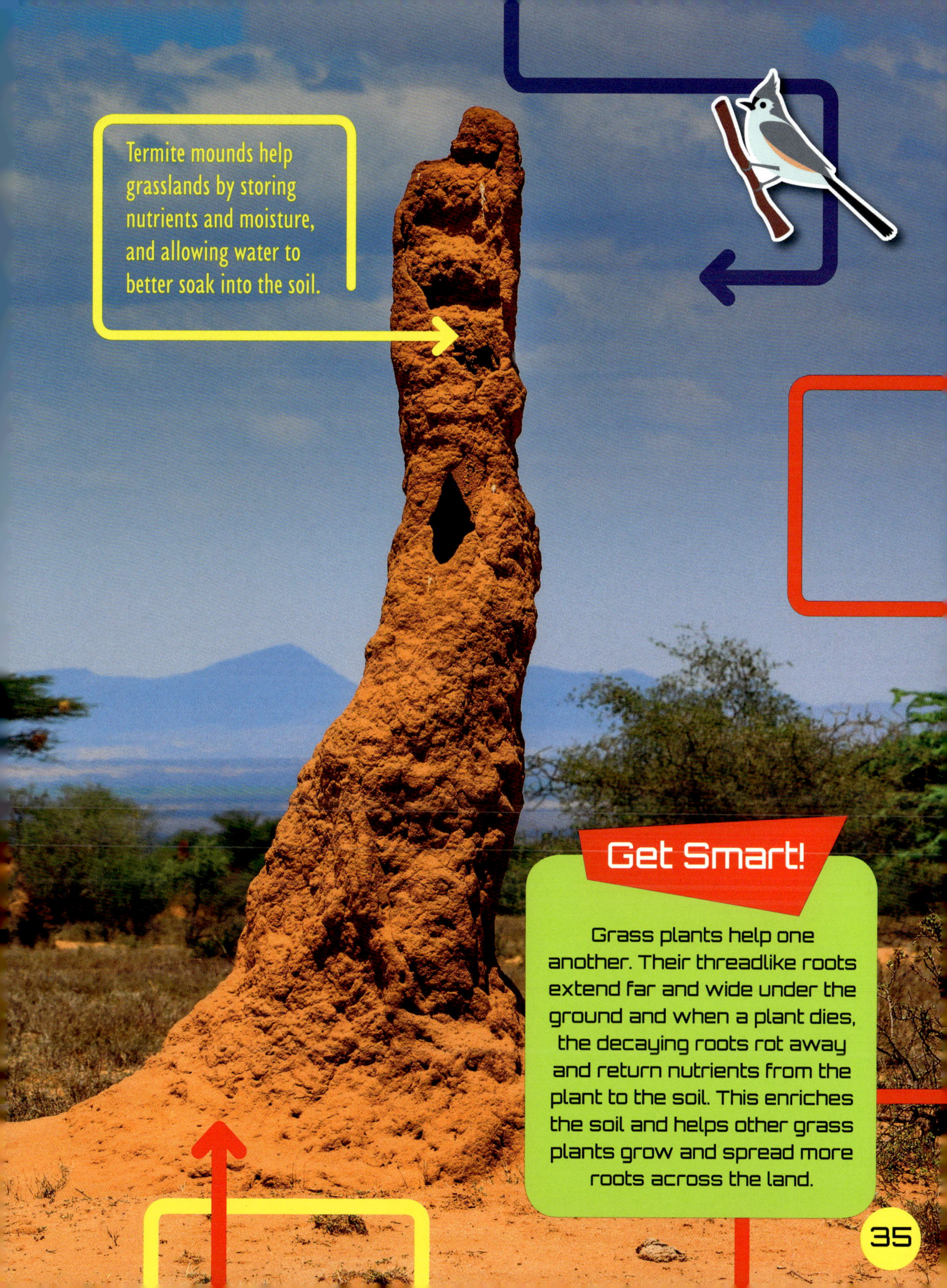

Termite mounds help grasslands by storing nutrients and moisture, and allowing water to better soak into the soil.

Get Smart!

Grass plants help one another. Their threadlike roots extend far and wide under the ground and when a plant dies, the decaying roots rot away and return nutrients from the plant to the soil. This enriches the soil and helps other grass plants grow and spread more roots across the land.

Keystone Species

Some animals have such a special and important impact on their ecosystem that they are known as **keystone species**. Keystone species are those that contribute so much to the life and health of the ecosystem that without them it would change drastically.

Prairie dogs are a keystone species. They live in groups in underground burrows. By digging deep tunnels with their sharp claws, they bring air into the soil to keep it healthy. They leave their droppings in deep chambers underground, which fertilizes the soil and helps plants grow. Prairie dogs trim the grass around burrows to help them spot predators, which keeps larger plants from taking over. Bison and other plant eaters rely on the grasses. Many predators, including coyotes, feed on the prairie dogs, too. Other animals such as burrowing owls also rely on prairie dog burrows for shelter.

Without prairie dogs living on the prairie, many aspects of prairie life would change or disappear.

Get Smart!

In some places, almost all the black-tailed prairie dogs have been poisoned, gassed, or shot. This has mainly been done by farmers who are worried that their cattle will break legs by stepping in the burrows. If this keystone species dies out, it would mean the loss of many other grassland species as well.

Elephants are a keystone species in tropical grasslands. When drought hits, elephants dig for water using their tusks. This provides water for other animals, too. Elephants eat shrubs and small trees, such as acacia, that grow on the savanna and keep them from taking over grasslands. Herds of elephants also create pathways through dense areas of shrubs as they feed. These pathways can be used by other animals, and they act as natural firebreaks to prevent a wildfire from spreading too far. Elephant dung also contains many seeds that grow into new grasses, bushes, and trees.

African elephants knock over trees on the savanna. This keeps the grassland from being taken over by trees.

Get flowchart smart!

How Prairie Dogs Help Prairies

Let's learn how prairie dogs help keep prairies healthy.

When prairie dogs dig deep tunnels with their sharp, thick claws, they bring air into the soil. This helps keep the soil healthy.

Other animals including burrowing owls rely on prairie dog burrows for shelter.

When prairie dogs leave their droppings in deep chambers underground, the waste fertilizes the soil and helps plants grow.

When prairie dogs trim the grass around their burrows to help them spot predators, it stops larger plants from taking over.

Bison and other plant eaters rely on the grasses that grow healthily around prairie dogs burrows.

Many grassland predators, including coyotes, eat prairie dogs.

Flowchart Smart

Chapter 6

The Future for Grassland Ecosystems

Grasslands are important ecosystems that contain an incredible variety of wildlife, but their future is under threat. Some grasslands are being altered and damaged by human activities.

Farmers have cleared many grasslands in order to create space to grow crops and raise **livestock**. People have also cleared grasslands to build towns and cities, golf courses, and other structures. Only about 1 percent of the North American wild prairie grasslands still exist. Most have been taken over by people for farms or towns. As their grassland homes are lost, the number of grassland animals decreases. Some animals are also threatened by hunting, such as African elephants, which are hunted for their valuable ivory tusks.

Huge areas of Earth's grasslands have been turned into farms, such as this one in Canada.

Get Smart!

Another problem facing grasslands is **climate change**. As parts of the world become hotter, the amount of rain that falls, and when it falls, also changes. Given that water is already in short supply in grasslands, this only increases the risk that grasslands will dry up completely and turn into deserts.

Some grasslands are damaged by overgrazing. This is when too many farm animals are allowed to graze an area. The animals eat all the plants and tug the plants up by their roots so they cannot regrow. After the blanket of grass has been destroyed, the fertile top layer of soil that was covered by the grass becomes drier. It turns to dust and blows away in the wind or gets washed away by rain. This leaves very dry land where hardly anything can grow. Overgrazing can sometimes even turn grasslands into deserts.

Wild bison once roamed North America in huge herds, but were hunted almost to **extinction**.

Get flowchart smart!

How Overgrazing Affects Grasslands

Find out how overgrazing can destroy a grassland.

Some farmers allow far too many farm animals to graze an area of wild grassland.

This leaves very dry land where hardly anything can grow.

Overgrazing can sometimes even turn grasslands into deserts.

The animals eat all the plants and tug the plants up by their roots so they cannot regrow.

After the blanket of grass is destroyed, the fertile top layer of soil begins to dry out.

The soil turns to dust and blows away or is washed away by rain.

Flowchart Smart

Protecting Grassland Ecosystems

Around the world, many governments, organizations, and individuals are trying to protect precious grassland ecosystems for the future.

Conservation groups raise public awareness of the problems grasslands face. They raise funds to pay for research and help governments turn grassland areas into wildlife **reserves** or **national parks**. In a national park or reserve, no one is allowed to damage the grasslands or do anything that can harm the wildlife. The Serengeti in Tanzania is a national park where the grasslands and their wildlife are protected by law.

Scientists attach tracking collars to grassland animals to find out more about how they live in grasslands.

People are also helping grasslands by planting trees around the edges of grasslands. These protect the grasslands from winds that could blow the fertile layer of topsoil away. Farmers help by leaving an area of land to recover and plants to regrow before allowing large herds of farm animals to graze it again. Individuals can help grasslands and other ecosystems around the world by doing what they can to combat climate change. They do this by trying to use less energy from fossil fuels. For example, walking instead of driving by car to use less fuel, and putting on a sweater instead of turning on the heat when they are cold. Grasslands are an amazing ecosystem, and we should do all we can to help them have a healthy future.

Get Smart!

Scientists work in grasslands gathering vital information that can help others figure out how to help these fragile ecosystems. They study threatened animals to see how they live and what they need. They look for ways to help farmers monitor areas of grassland plants so they can tell when they need to move farm livestock from the areas.

These herds of zebras and buffalo live safely in Serengeti National Park.

Glossary

adaptations Changes to suit a new situation.

bacteria Tiny living things that can help decompose waste.

camouflage The ability to blend in with the surroundings.

carbon dioxide A gas in the air.

climate change A change in the pattern of the world's weather caused by Earth's atmosphere getting warmer.

conservation The act of guarding, protecting, or preserving something.

decomposers Living things that break down waste.

desert An area of dry land where there is almost no water or rain.

digest Break down food in the body and obtain nutrients from it.

dormant Inactive or resting.

drought A long period of time with little or no rain.

ecosystems The living and nonliving things in a place, interacting with one another.

evaporation Turning from a liquid to a gas.

extinction Died out completely.

fertilizer A substance that helps plants grow.

food web The feeding relationships between living things in an ecosystem.

herds Large groups of grazing animals.

interacting Acting in such a way as to have an effect on one another.

keystone species A living thing that is very important to an ecosystem.

livestock Farm animals.

national parks Areas in nature where the wildlife is protected by law.

nutrients Substances that living things need to survive and grow.

photosynthesis The process by which green plants make sugary food using the energy in sunlight.

predators Animals that catch and eat other animals.

prey An animal hunted and eaten by another animal.

proboscis A long, sucking mouthpart.

recycling Converting waste into something new.

reserves Protected areas to keep living things and landscapes of special interest safe from destruction.

resources Something found in nature that is useful, such as plants and water.

species Types of living things.

temperate Found in places with a moderate range of temperatures.

tropical Found in places near the equator, which are warm all year round.

For More Information

Books

Bjorklund, Ruth. *24 Hours in a Grassland* (Day in an Ecosystem). New York, NY: Cavendish Square Publishing, 2017.

Dickmann, Nancy. *Map and Track Grasslands* (Map and Track Biomes and Animals). New York, NY: Crabtree Publishing Company, 2019.

Gagne, Tammy. *Grassland Ecosystems* (Earth's Ecosystems). Mankato, MN: 12-Story Library, 2018.

Smalls, June. *We Need Prairie Dogs* (Animal Files). Mendota Heights, MN: Focus Readers, 2019.

Websites

Go on a mission to find out more about grasslands at:
earthobservatory.nasa.gov/experiments/biome/biograssland.php

Read more about grasslands at:
kids.nceas.ucsb.edu/biomes/grassland.html

Discover more about grassland ecosystems at
https://www.nationalgeographic.com/environment/habitats/grasslands

For grassland maps, species, and more visit:
w3.marietta.edu/~biol/biomes/grass.htm

Index